The Best GRANDFATHER NAMES Ever

CHOOSE YOUR PERFECT GRANDPA NAME,
from Papa to Nonno and Beyond!

CATHY LIVINGSTONE

sourcebook

T0016566

Published by Sourcebooks
P.O. Box 4410, Naperville, Illinois 60567–4410
(630) 961-3900
sourcebooks.com

Cataloging-in-Publication Data is on file with the Library of Congress.

Printed and bound in the United States of America.
SB 10 9 8 7 6 5 4 3 2 1

CONTENTS

FOREWORD

Bubbe, my Irish Catholic mother, unknowingly initiated the idea for this book. When our daughter was born, my mother announced that she would not be called "Grandma" by her grandchildren, but "Bubbe." My siblings and I thought it was quite comical, since Bubbe is a traditional Jewish grandmother name and we are Catholic. However, the name actually seemed fitting, even though we didn't know the true definition of the name Bubbe. Notwithstanding any criticism or input from us, my mother prevailed, and Bubbe Caputo was born.

Not to be outdone, my father became Grandpa Colonel.

INTRODUCTION

No two grandfathers are alike. Therefore, why not have a helpful book to assist you in choosing the best name for you? Today's grandpas are active, involved, complex, loving, and heroic. And grandpas are playing a significant role in their grandchildren's lives every day. It is important that your grandfather name defines the unique, wonderful grandfather that you are.

The following descriptions of grandfatherly names were derived from many sources: from various grandfather stories people shared with me, online grandparent blogs, and my imagination to create light-hearted and entertaining descriptions. Hence, every grandfather name is subject to your creativity, perception, and real-life experiences.

Whether you are already a grandfather or a grandfather-to-be, many congratulations to you! May this book bring you some laughs and fun moments with your family and friends. Best wishes for a joyous and adventurous grandfatherhood!

> "A baby has a way of making a man out of his father and a boy out of his grandfather."
>
> —Angie Papadakis

Grandpa Name Quiz

Congratulations on your upcoming grandfatherhood journey! Your first exciting step is choosing your special new grandpa name. Your grandpa name is important because you are unique and special—there's only one you! This quiz will start you on your way to finding the perfect name for you.

You drive a:

- **A.** convertible or sports car
- **B.** pickup truck
- **C.** hybrid
- **D.** Cadillac, Buick, or four-door sedan

In your leisure time, you usually:

- **A.** trade stocks
- **B.** play golf or pickup basketball
- **C.** watch sports on TV
- **D.** read

Your best friend would say your best quality is:

A. your sense of style

B. your sense of smell

C. your sense of humor

D. your sense of direction

Your favorite vacation is:

A. a weekend away with the boys

B. downhill skiing in the Rockies

C. camping in the middle of nowhere

D. sunning yourself at the beach

Your everyday dress style is mostly:

A. sports teams logo attire

B. casual—khakis, jeans, and athleisure wear

C. loud, bold colorful clothes

D. a shirt and tie

Your favorite sport is:

A. football or ice hockey

B. track and field

C. bowling or curling

D. chess

At an amusement park, you would:

A. shoot the ducks, because you like hunting

B. jump into a bumper car

C. hit the roller coaster

D. skip the rides and go directly to the karaoke

In the movie of your life, you'd be played by:

A. Al Pacino

B. Harrison Ford

C. Steve Carell

D. Denzel Washington

Your favorite kind of house pet is a:

A. dog

B. cat

C. parakeet

D. goldfish

For Halloween, you like to dress up as:

A. Hugh Hefner

B. a farmer

C. a rock star

D. Abe Lincoln

If you were in a music competition, you would sing:

A. "A Hard Day's Night"

B. "We Are the Champions"

C. "(I Can't Get No) Satisfaction"

D. "Born in the USA"

Answers

Mostly A

You are very social and outgoing, and you love large gatherings. Possible Grandpa names for you are: Glampa, G-Man, Grampy, PoPo, or Pops.

Mostly B

You are active and adventurous, and enjoy the outdoors. Possible Grandpa names for you are: Big Daddy, Champ, Chief, Grandad, or Lito.

Mostly C

You are a comedian who loves telling stories and tall tales. Possible Grandpa names for you are: Grandmaster, G-Pa, Papa Bear, Popz, or Ye Ye.

Mostly D

You are serious, trustworthy, and wise. Possible Grandpa names for you are: Gramps, Papa, Pepe, Opa, or Zeyde.

> "Great fathers get promoted
> to Grandfathers."
>
> —Joseph Marshall III

GRANDFATHER NAMES

A

Abuelo

(pronounced bä-lō). Literally Spanish for "grandfather." He has never colored his wavy salt-and-pepper hair.
Persona: Good-Looking Spanish Grandpa

Ace

(pronounced ās). 1. A winning tennis serve. 2. A man who wears embarrassingly short, white tennis shorts.
Persona: Don't-Really-Care-What-I-Look-Like Grandpa
Fun Fact: The "Dream of Aces" card trick has become one of the most famous card tricks of all time.

Atuk	**(pronounced a-tōōk).** The word from the from Inuit Eskimo language for "beautiful father." **Persona:** Beautiful Inuit Grandpa
Avo	**(pronounced āvō).** Masculine, tough grandfather. Never took a handout in his life. **Persona:** Hardworking Portuguese Grandpa

Baba	**(pronounced bä-bä).** Can see all the magic and wonder of the world through his grandchildren's eyes. **Persona:** Let's-Go-Build-a-Go-Cart Grandpa
Babar	**(pronounced bä-bär).** He has mighty strength. **Persona:** Protective Grandpa **Fun Fact:** Babar the Elephant is an elephant character who first appeared in 1931 in the French children's book *Histoire de Babar*.

Bear	**(pronounced bâr).** Big, brawny on the outside, but soft on the inside. **Persona:** Walks-Softly-but-Carries-a-Big-Stick Grandpa **Fun Fact:** Chief Standing Bear was the famous and most feared chief of the Ponca Native Americans (1829–1908).
Big D	**(pronounced big dē).** Former college football player. **Persona:** Almost-Pro Grandpa
Big Daddy	**(pronounced bĭg dăd-ē).** His belly shakes when he laughs. **Persona:** Larger-than-Life Grandpa
Bo	**(pronounced bō).** Loves his grits-n-gravy breakfast. **Persona:** Southern-Born Grandpa
Bogey	**(pronounced bō-gē).** Someone who's always late for every family event. **Persona:** Just-Let-Me-Finish-One-More-Thing Grandpa.

Boomer

(pronounced boom-r). He often has a loud, booming voice.

Persona: Loud Grandpa

Fun Fact: Former NFL quarterback Norman Julius "Boomer" Esiason's grandpa name is "Boompa."

> "You've got to do your own growing, no matter how tall your grandfather was."
>
> *—Tony Dungy*

Boss

(pronounced bôs). Watchful, judgmental grandfather.

Persona: Never-Misses-a-Move Grandpa

Fun Fact: The greedy, unethical commissioner on the TV sitcom *The Dukes of Hazzard* was Boss Hogg.

Bub

(pronounced bŭb). He's a helpful grandfather.

Persona: Tinkering Grandpa

Fun Fact: The grandfather on the 1960s TV sitcom *My Three Sons* was called Bub.

Bubba	**(pronounced bŭb-bä).** A Southern U.S. slang word loosely translated as "good ole Southern boy." **Persona:** Soft-Southern-Drawl Grandpa **Fun Fact:** Former president Bill Clinton's childhood nickname was Bubba.
Buck	**(pronounced bŭk).** Old cowboy movies are an obsession for Buck, especially those starring actor John Wayne. **Persona:** Cowboy Grandpa **Fun Fact:** Buck Brannaman is the real-life horse whisperer.
Bud	**(pronounced bŭd).** 1. Flower or blossom. 2. A man who enjoys Bud Light beer. **Persona:** Middle-Class, Hardworking American Grandpa **Fun Fact:** The nickname "Bud" may have derived from the Scottish Gaelic word "Bhodaich" which translates in English to "Old Man."

Buddy

(pronounced bŭd-ē). He is your best friend.

Persona: Loyal Grandpa

Fun Fact: Buddy is the third-most-popular male dog name.

Bumpa

(pronounced bŭm-pä). He loves his La-Z-Boy recliner.

Persona: Slow-Moving Grandpa

Buyuk Baba

(pronounced bī-uk bä-bä). He is reserved and quiet. He likes to take long walks around town.

Persona: Nomadic Turkish Grandfather

Captain

(pronounced kăp-tn). 1. Commander of a ship. 2. A man who believes he is the commander of his home.

Persona: Supervisory Grandpa

Famous TV Characters: Captain Stubing, Captain Kangaroo.

Champ	**(pronounced champ).** He likes winning—even against his grandkids. **Persona:** Competitive Grandpa
Chickie	**(pronounced chĭk-ē).** Ready to make a beer run at a moment's notice. **Persona:** Good-Hearted Grandpa **Fun Fact:** Chickie Donohue, eighty-two as of writing, made a brave, unannounced trip to Vietnam in 1968 to bring his New York soldier friends a beer and a hug of support.
Chief	**(pronounced chēf).** Like a fire chief, he is able to put out family fires quickly. **Persona:** One Hot Grandpa
Coach	**(pronounced kōch).** 1. Teacher, instructor. 2. One who is affable off the field and tyrannical on the field. **Persona:** Every-Moment-Is-a-Teachable-Moment Grandpa **Famous TV Character:** Lovable Ernie "Coach" Pantusso from TV sitcom *Cheers*.

Colonel	**(pronounced kûr-nl).** 1. Military rank of a commissioned officer. 2. One who is proud to have served his country. **Persona:** Chest-High-Shoulders-Back Grandpa
Crackers	**(pronounced krăk-rs).** The years of nagging are starting to make him a bit "crackers." **Persona:** Hanging-in-There Grandpa

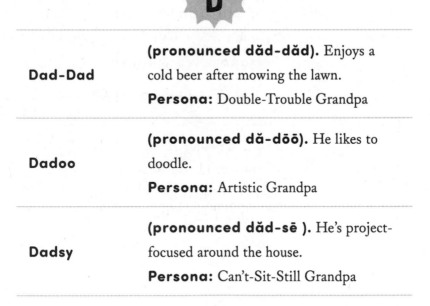

Dad-Dad	**(pronounced dăd-dăd).** Enjoys a cold beer after mowing the lawn. **Persona:** Double-Trouble Grandpa
Dadoo	**(pronounced dă-dōō).** He likes to doodle. **Persona:** Artistic Grandpa
Dadsy	**(pronounced dăd-sē).** He's project-focused around the house. **Persona:** Can't-Sit-Still Grandpa

Dappy	**(pronounced dăp-pē).** He's trim and neat. **Persona:** Stylish Grandpa
Dedyshka	**(pronounced dĕd-ĭsh-kä).** Loves big family gatherings. **Persona:** Big Russian Grandpa
Doc	**(pronounced dŏc).** Able to solve all problems. **Persona:** Comforting Grandpa **Fun Fact:** John Henry Holliday, better known as Doc Holliday, was an Old West gambler and gunslinger.
Domino	**(pronounced däm-ĭ-nō).** He has an assertive personality. **Persona:** Domineering Grandpa
Duke	**(pronounced dōōk).** 1. A nobleman with the highest hereditary rank. 2. One very proud of his ancestry and offspring. **Persona:** Honorable Grandpa

Farfar

(pronounced fär-fär). Literally translated from the Swedish language as "father's father."
Persona: Fair-Skinned Swedish Grandpa
Fun Fact: In 1951, Sweden's Gustave Hakansson became famous after winning the Sverigeloppet, a one-thousand-mile bicycle race covering the length of Sweden, at age sixty-six. He then became known as the "Steel Grandfather."

Faux Pa

(pronounced fō pä). Embarrassing social mistakes are common with Faux Pa.
Persona: Socially Awkward Grandpa

Fly

(pronounced flī). One definition of the word "fly" is "to engage in flight." He never stays in one place for very long.
Persona: On-the-Go Grandpa
Fun Fact: Fly-fishing is growing in popularity with the ladies.

Geepa	**(pronounced gĕ-pä).** You always feel better after talking with Geepa. **Persona:** Positive Grandpa
GeePee	**(pronounced gĕ-pĕ).** Fond of tickling his grandkids. **Persona:** Happy Grandpa
Glampa	**(pronounced glăm-pä).** His classic good looks and strong physique make him seem like a movie star. **Persona:** Hollywood Grandpa
G-Man	**(pronounced jē-man).** He is very sure of himself. **Persona:** Confident Grandpa
Godfather	**(pronounced gŏd-fä-thr).** If you look like Marlon Brando and have a family business…then Godfather it is. **Persona:** Dark-Suit-Wearing Italian Grandpa **Fun Fact:** *The Godfather* movies depict the fictitious Corleone crime family from the 1900s through the 1980s. Marlon Brando won an Oscar for his portrayal of Don Corleone, the Godfather.

G-Pa	**(pronounced jē-pä).** An instigator who loves riling up the grandchildren. **Persona:** Crazy Grandpa
Gramps	**(pronounced grămps).** Informal name for grandfather. **Persona:** Nice Grandpa **Famous TV Characters:** The grandfather on the 1970s TV show *Lassie* was called Gramps.
Grampy	**(pronounced grăm-pē).** Can always fix a broken bike. **Persona:** Just-Let-Me-Take-a-Look-Here Grandpa
Grand Poppa	**(pronounced grănd pŏp-pä).** He's calm and composed under pressure. **Persona:** Cool-as-a-Cucumber Grandpa
Grandad	**(pronounced grăn-dăd).** He has not missed a Sunday church sermon in over forty years. **Persona:** Good Ole Religious Grandpa
Grand-D	**(pronounced grănd-dē).** He is a highly self-respecting man. **Persona:** Dignified Grandpa

Grandfather

(pronounced grănd-fä-thr). He is somewhat standoffish around small children.

Persona: Formal Grandpa

"A grandfather is someone with silver in his hair and gold in his heart."

—*Unknown*

Grandmaster

(pronounced grănd-ma-str). He had a successful career.

Persona: Hardworking Grandpa

Fun Fact: Grandmaster Flash is considered one of the pioneers of hip-hop DJing. This is also the highest chess title.

Grandpa

(pronounced grănd-pä). Easygoing and likable.

Persona: Just-Call-Me Grandpa

Fun Fact: Grandpa Munster, from the 1960s TV sitcom *The Munsters*, could turn himself into a bat.

Grandpapa	**(pronounced grănd-pä-pä).** Enjoys taking the grandkids to the beach for a swim. **Persona:** Not-Afraid-to-Swim-with-the-Sharks Grandpa **Fun Fact:** One of the most famous sea explorers in the world, Jacques Cousteau, was called Papa Grand—a fun twist on Grandpapa.
Grandpaw	**(pronounced grănd-pô).** With his deep southern drawl, he can capture an audience with his raucous boyhood stories. **Persona:** Deep-South Grandpa
Grandpee	**(pronounced grăn-pē).** No matter how many designer shirts or pants he is given, he never fails to look unfashionable. **Persona:** Fashion-Isn't-His-Thing Grandpa
Grandude	**(pronounced grăn-dōōd).** Highest level of cool. **Persona:** Cool-and-Collected Grandpa **Fun Fact:** Paul McCartney's grandkids call him Grandude.

Grandy	**(pronounced grăn-dē).** He can fix almost anything. **Persona:** Handy Grandpa
Granite	**(pronounced grăn-it).** Still has rock-hard biceps. **Persona:** Workout Grandpa
Grootpapa	**(pronounced grōōt-pa-pa).** Big, sturdy, and surprisingly open-minded. **Persona:** Fair-and-Impartial Grandpa
Grootvader	**(pronounced grōōt-väd-r).** Passionate about brewing his own signature beer in the garage. **Persona:** Gotta-Have-a-Hobby DutchGrandpa **Fun Fact:** had to be top-fermented.
Grumpa	**(pronounced grŭm-pä).** Worries about the stock market daily. **Persona:** Financial Grandpa

Grumpy	**(pronounced grŭm-pē).** Does not like it when family events are scheduled during football season. **Persona:** Former-High-School-Football-Player Grandpa
Gubbe	**(pronounced gŭb-bē).** Grandpa version of Bubbe. **Persona:** Agreeable Grandpa
Guppy	**(pronounced gŭp-pē).** He likes to spend his time fishing. **Persona:** Fisherman Grandpa

> "Grandfathers are just antique little boys."
>
> —*Unknown*

Halaboji	**(pronounced hăl-ä-bŭ-jē).** Chooses his words carefully. **Persona:** Man-of-Few-Words Korean Grandpa
Hampa	**(pronounced hăm-pä).** He's one handsome grampa. **Persona:** Handsome Grampa
Herr	**(pronounced her).** He is such a gentleman. **Persona:** Noble Grandpa

Itsy	**(pronounced ĭt-sē).** One who is willing to see the big picture. He doesn't sweat the small stuff. **Persona:** Optimistic Grandpa

Jumpy

(pronounced jŭm-pē). Jumpy takes a little something before the grandchildren come over.

Persona: Likes-It-on-the-Quiet-Side Grandpa

King

(pronounced kĭng). Thinks he is king of the castle.

Persona: High-and-Mighty Grandpa

Fun Fact: The tomb of King Tut, the Egyptian pharaoh, was discovered in 1922. Over three thousand years old, the tomb contained golden riches.

Lito	**(pronounced lē-tō).** His handlebar mustache is starting to gray. **Persona:** Mustache-Twisting Grandpa
Lolo	**(pronounced lō-lō).** Can float in the pool for hours. **Persona:** Light-as-a-Feather Filipino Grandpa
Lumpy	**(pronounced lŭm-pē).** Too many nights spent watching TV has made Grampa a bit "lumpy." **Persona:** Late-Night-TV Grandpa

Mate	**(pronounced māt).** Still adores his mate after all these years. **Persona:** He-Only-Has-Eyes-for-Her Grandpa

Mepaw	**(pronounced mē-pä).** Loose Southern slang for "my father." **Persona:** Can-Still-Drive-That-John-Deere-Tractor Grandpa
Morfar	**(pronounced mōr-fär).** Literally translates from Swedish as "mother's father." **Persona:** Blond-Headed Swedish Grandpa

Nonno	**(pronounced nŏn-nō).** He claims his "meat-a-balls" have no competition. They are the world's best. **Persona:** Apron-Wearing Italian Grandpa **Fun Fact:** Nonni's Italian Eatery (in Concord, New Hampshire) created the world's largest edible meatball in 2009. It weighed 222.5 pounds and was certified by the *Guinness Book of World Records*.

O

Oji-chan	**(pronounced oji-chän).** Drives very slowly and carefully. **Persona:** Takes-One-Day-at-a-Time Japanese Grandpa
Opa	**(pronounced ō-pä).** Card tricks and board games are his specialty. **Persona:** Fun German Grandpa **Fun Fact:** Arnold Alois Schwarzenegger is an Austrian-American former professional bodybuilder, actor, model, businessman, and politician who served as the thirty eighth governor of California. His grandkids call him "Opa."

P

Pa	**(pronounced pä).** Likes to wear his old, broken-in cowboy hat. **Persona:** Cowboy Grandpa
Papa	**(pronounced pä-pä).** You always feel safe and loved when you are with Papa. **Persona:** Best Kind of Grandpa

Papa Bear	**(pronounced pä-pä ber).** Fiercely protective of his family. **Persona:** Overbearing Grandpa
Papa Daddy	**(pronounced pä-pä da-dē).** He's not ready to become a grandpa. **Persona:** Reluctant Grandpa
Papaw	**(pronounced pä-pô).** Willing to teach each of his grandchildren how to duck hunt. **Persona:** Loaded Gun Grandpa **Fun Fact:** Papaw is the most commonly used name for Grandpa in Alabama, West Virginia, Louisiana, and Mississippi.
Papi	**(pronounced păp-pē).** He's one happy papi. **Persona:** Always-in-High-Spirits Grandpa **Fun Fact:** David "Big Papi" Ortiz was the designated hitter for the Boston Red Sox. His batting helped the team win their 2004, 2007, and 2013 World Series Championships.

PaPoo	**(pronounced pă-pōō).** His RV displays all the stickers from the campgrounds he's visited. **Persona:** Enjoying-Retired-Life Grandpa
Pappous	**(pronounced pă-pōōs).** Will drive over an hour to his favorite Greek restaurant. **Persona:** Loves-His-Old-Country Greek Grandpa **Fun Fact:** An "eggoni" is a grandchild of a pappous.
Paw	**(pronounced pô).** His family has been growing tobacco for generations. **Persona:** Got-a-Light Grandpa
Pepe	**(pronounced pĕ-pä).** He's constantly on the quest for love. **Persona:** Romantic Grandpa
Pepere	**(pronounced pĕp-âr).** Bow-tie-wearing grandfather. **Persona:** Serious French Grandpa

Pickles
(pronounced pĭk-ls). At any time, he can be either slick, prickly, or very sour.
Persona: Hard-to-Understand Grandpa

"Hunger is the best pickle."
—Ben Franklin

Picky
(pronounced pĭk-ēē). He tends to debate petty issues.
Persona: Picky Grandpa

Pilot
(pronounced pī-lət). He is easygoing and takes care of himself.
Persona: Willing-to-Try-New-Things Grandpa

Pop
(pronounced pŏp). He is warm and cheerful.
Persona: Friendly Grandpa

PoPo
(pronounced pŏ-pō). He likes his house nice and orderly.
Persona: Controlling Grandpa

Poppi	**(pronounced pŏp-pē).** He is helpful around the house and yard. **Persona:** Tool-Belt-Wearing Grandpa **Fun Fact:** Poppy seeds are an oilseed obtained from the opium poppy.
Pop Pop	**(pronounced pŏp pŏp).** He's a grandpa who is twice the fun. **Persona:** Popular Grandpa
Popsie	**(pronounced pop-sē).** Whimsical version of Pop. **Persona:** Playful and Mischievous Grandpa
Popz	**(pronounced pŏp-zē).** He likes to listen to disco-rap music. **Persona:** Hip-Hop Grandpa
Puff	**(pronounced pŭff).** He is just like a cream puff. Hard on the outside, but soft on the inside. **Persona:** Old-Softy Grandpa

Radar

(pronounced rādär). Former army sergeant who can handily watch the grandchildren—his innate radar can detect their presence, direction, distance, and speed!
Persona: Army Grandpa

River

(pronounced riv-r). He goes with the flow.
Persona: Old-Man-River Grandpa
Fun Fact: The Mississippi River is often called "Old Man River."

Rock

(pronounced räk). Tough and usually unwilling to bend.
Persona: Headstrong Grandpa

Rocky

(pronounced räk-ē). Always quick with a playful jab.
Persona: Boxing Grandpa
Fun Fact: Robert "Rocky" Balboa is the heavyweight southpaw boxer in the *Rocky* film series portrayed by Sylvester Stallone. There are six *Rocky* films (1976–2006).

Scratchy	**(pronounced skra-chē).** Grandkids don't like his scratchy beard. **Persona:** Gave-Up-His-Razor-Long-Ago Grandpa
Seanathair	**(pronounced shăn-a-hr).** Still has all his freckles and boyish good looks. **Persona:** Irish Grandpa
Skipper	**(pronounced skĭp-r).** He is good at bossing people around. **Persona:** Seafaring Grandpa **Famous TV Characters:** The Skipper was the captain of the SS *Minnow* and the leader on the 1960s *Gilligan's Island* TV show.
Sonny	**(pronounced sŭn-ē).** He's someone who's had many different and interesting careers. **Persona:** Sweet-Singing Grandpa **Fun Fact:** Sonny and Cher (Bono) were an American pop music duo in the 1970s. Sonny Bono was a singer, entertainer, actor, record producer, and politician.

Sumo

(pronounced sōō-mō). He has a very slow but deliberate gait.

Persona: Short and Thick Grandpa

Fun Fact: Sumo is a stylized form of Japanese wrestling.

Tank

(pronounced tank). He has an aggressive personality.

Persona: Combative Grandpa

Tiger

(pronounced tī-gr). He greets you with gentle jabs and punches.

Persona: Pretend-Boxer Grandpa

Tug

(pronounced tug). Likes to quote positive, uplifting phrases.

Persona: Rallying-Cry Grandpa

Fun Fact: Frank Edwin "Tug" McGraw Jr. was a professional Major League Baseball player and father to country singer Tim McGraw.

Tutu Kane

(pronounced tōō-tōō-kān). He has a peaceful and calm spirit.

Persona: Supernatural Grandpa

Ye Ye

(pronounced yē-yē). Faithfully does his chores every day.
Persona: Hardworking-Till-the-End Chinese Grandpa

Zeyde

(pronounced zā-dē). Happy and willing to take direction from Bubbe. He likes to keep the peace.
Persona: Peacemaker Jewish Grandpa

"Seventy-two percent think being a grandparent is the single most important role in their lives."
—*Grandkidsmatter.org*

CELEBRITY GRANDPAS

CELEBRITY GRANDPA	CELEBRITY GRANDPA NAME
Michael Douglas	Bubba
Former president George W. Bush	El Jefe (the boss)
Nelson Mandela	Grandad
Flavor Flav	Grandaddy
Jim Carey	Granddaddy Jim
Lester Holt	Granddude

Michael Jordan	**Grandpa**
Snoop Dog	**Grandpa**
Damon Wayans	**Grandpapa**
Jacques Cousteau	**Papa Grand**
Paul McCartney	**Grandude**
Arnold Schwarzenegger	**Opa**
Ozzy Osbourne	**Papa**
Steven Tyler	**Papa Stevie**
Tom Hanks	**Papou**

Martin Sheen	**Peach**
Alice Cooper	**Pop Pop**
Former president Bill Clinton	**Pop Pop**
Lionel Richie	**Pop Pop**
Cedric the Entertainer	**Popsy**
Former Australian prime minister Malcolm Turnbull	**Yeye and Baba**

"Grandfathers give us not only wisdom
and encouragement, but they are
an inspiration to us."

— *Kate Summers*

GRANDFATHER STORIES

PRIME MINISTER

Former Australian prime minister Malcolm Turnbull has two grandpa names! He is Yeye to one grandchild and Baba to his other two grandchildren.

LULU-PAPA

Grandma's name was Lucy, but her husband of forty-eight years always called her Lulu, and so did her grandchildren. Then Lulu decided to rename her husband from Grandpa to Papa because she thought "Lulu and Papa" sounded better!

LOLLY-POP

One witty grandma decided that, since grandpa was going to be Pop, she would be Lolly, making them Lolly-Pop.

GRAMPS MORGAN

Roy "Gramps" Morgan is a Jamaican singer, instrumentalist, producer, record executive, and entrepreneur. He is known by the name of Gramps. (For more, see: GrampsMorgan.com.)

GRANDFATHER MOUNTAIN

Grandfathers even have their own mountain named after them! Grandfather Mountain is a mountain, a non-profit attraction, and a North Carolina state park near Linville, North Carolina.

AMAZING GRANDPAS

OLDEST GRANDPA FIREFIGHTER

On his way to turning 110 in 2024, Vincent Dransfield lives alone, is completely independent, and is also an active volunteer firefighter in Little Falls, NJ.

ATHLETIC GRANDPA

Otto Thaning, a seventy-three-year-old South African heart surgeon, became the oldest person to swim the English Channel in 2014. Mr. Thaning trained medically under Dr. Christian Barnard, who performed the world's first successful human-to-human heart transplant in 1967.

GRANDFATHER OF ROCK 'N' ROLL

Robert Johnson, an American blues singer, guitarist, and songwriter (1911–1938), is among the most famous of Delta blues musicians. He ranked fifth in *Rolling Stone*'s list of the "100 Greatest Guitarists of All Time" and is considered by some to be the grandfather of Rock 'n' Roll.

PAUL MCCARTNEY, SONGWRITER AND AUTHOR

The number-one *New York Times* bestselling picture book adventure *Hey Grandude*, about a group of children's adventures with their grandpa, was written by Paul McCartney. He has written two Grandude books, the other being *Grandude's Green Submarine*.

Grandparents spend $179 billion per year on their grandkids.

INTERNATIONAL GRANDFATHER NAMES

AFRICAN LANGUAGES

Babu (Swahili)

Oupa (Afrikaans)

Tatekulu (Oshiwambo)

ARABIC

Jadd

ARMENIAN

Papik

BOSNIAN

Deda

Djed

CHINESE

Wai Zufu (maternal)

Ye Ye (paternal)

Zufu (paternal)

CZECH

Deda

Dedecek

DANISH

Bedstefar

FLEMISH

Bompa

DUTCH

Grootvader

Opa

FRENCH

Grand Père

Pepe

Pepere

FIJIAN

Buqu

Tukaqu

GERMAN

Grossvader

Grossvater

Opa

FILIPINO

Lolo

FINNISH

Isoisä

GREEK

Papa

Papou

Pappo

Pappouli

Pappous

HAWAIIAN

Kapuna Kane

Tutu Kane

HEBREW

Saba

Zeyde

HINDI

Daada

Dadi

HUNGARIAN

Nagypapa

ICELANDIC

Afi

INDONESIAN

Kakek

IRISH

Athair Ciallmhar

Daideo

Seanathair

ITALIAN

Nonnino

Nonno

JAPANESE

Ojiisan (formal)

Sofu (informal)

KOREAN

Hal-abeoji

NATIVE ALASKAN

Adax (Aleut dialect)

Ataataga Ataataga

  (Eskimo, Inupiaq dialect)

NATIVE AMERICAN LANGUAGES

Agiduda (Cherokee)

Eduda (Cherokee)

Gaka (Lakota)

NORWEGIAN

Bestefar

Far Far

Mor Far

POLISH

Dziadak

PORTUGUESE

Avô Avô

ROMANIAN

Bunic

Bunicul

RUSSIAN

Dedushka

SCOTTISH

Seanair

SERBIAN

Deda

SOUTH INDIAN

Dada

Taata (Telegu)

TURKISH

Buyuk Baba

Dede

SPANISH

Abuelo

Lito

Lolo

Papi

UKRAINIAN

Deda

Didus

VIETNAMESE

Ông Nội

SWEDISH

Farfar

Mor-Far

YIDDISH

Zadie

Zayde

Zeyde

TAIWANESE

A-Gong

"To a small child, the perfect granddad is unafraid of big dogs and fierce storms but absolutely terrified of the word 'boo.'"

—Robert Brault

GRANDFATHER NAMES BY PERSONALITY

CLASSY

Dappy

Doc

Duke

Grand Poppa

Grandad

Herr

FUN

Baba

Bear

Buddy

Dadoo

Faux Pa

Geepa

ENERGETIC

Big Daddy

Boomer

Chickie

Crackers

Grampy

Gubbe

HIP

Glampa

Grandmaster

Grandude

Grandy

Pop Pop

Popz

ROMANTIC

Abuelo

Hampa

Lito

Nonno

Pepe

Pepere

STOIC

Avo

Dedyshka

Grand-D

Grandfather

Grootpapa

Paw

SOCIAL

Abuelo

Bo

Bud

Dadsy

G-Pa

Sonny

TOUGH

Big D

Boss

Chief

Colonel

Godfather

Rocky

SPORTS GUY

Ace

Bogey

Captain

Champ

Coach

Sumo

TRADITIONAL

Grandpa

Grandpaw

Morfar

Opa

Papa

Pop

PERFECT PAIRS

GRANDMA AND GRANDPA NAMES
THAT GO TOGETHER PERFECTLY

Airy—Ace	Gigi—Poppi
Bebe—Bear	Glamma—Glampa
Birdie—Bogey	Gram—Crackers
Bitsy—Itsy	Granny—Grampy
Bossie—Boss	Happy—Grumpy
Bubbe—Zeyde	Huggie—Bear
Chickie—Coach	Indy—Chief
Chickie—Farfar	Jumpy—Lumpy
Cici—Captain	Juno—Jupiter
Coco—Puff	Lolly—Pop
Dame—Duke	Lucy—Ricky
Didi—Baba	MeMaw—Mepaw
Ditti—Doc	Mimi—Ace
Duchess—Duke	Mimi—Mate
Gigi—Gramps	MopMop—Pop Pop

Nana—Papa

Nanoo—PaPoo

Queenie—Ace

Queenie—King

Sassy—Pappy

Sugar—Big Daddy

Tickles—Pickles

YaYa—PaPa

"Enjoy the little things, for one day
you may look back and realize they were
the big things."

—*Robert Brault*

GRANDPA'S GRANDBABY PLANNER

When it comes to something as important as a new grandbaby, it is always a good idea to be as organized as possible before arrival. The following checklist is a super helpful tool to ensure you are ready for the big day and the days following shortly after!

1-3 months prior to baby's due date

☐ Find out the date of the "baby" shower and mark your calendar.

- Review the baby registry and purchase item(s).
- Find your son or daughter's favorite old baby blanket, rattle, stuffed animal, etc., to share and/ or gift to the parent as a wonderful memento of when they were a baby.

- [ ] Inquire if a baby "reveal" party is also planned. If yes, find out the date.
- [ ] Make sure your house is equipped with all the necessary gear you'll need to babysit your new grandchild.

EQUIPMENT

- Portable crib (Pack 'n Play)
- Car seat (convertible from infant to toddler)
- Exersaucer
- High chair
- Bouncy seat
- Stroller
- Baby gate

ACCESSORIES

- Bibs
- Burp cloths
- Baby blankets
- Diapers
- Diaper wipes warmer
- Changing pad
- Thermometer
- Breakproof bowls and spoons
- White noise machine
- Books, toys, stuffed animals

- [ ] Wash and clean all new baby equipment and accessories.

One week prior to due date

☐ Make sure you understand the birth plan and ask nicely how you can help.

☐ Find old baby photos or the baby book of your son or daughter when they were born.

☐ Make sure you fully understand how to take photos with your phone or iPad; practice.

☐ Update phone contact list—family, friends, neighbors.

☐ Create text groups for easy texting about baby's arrival!

☐ Buy an extra phone charger to always carry with you and your phone.

☐ Make sure you fully understand how to text and email new baby photos to family and friends.

☐ Install infant car seat—be ready!

- Go to local fire station for infant car seat inspection (to make sure it's installed correctly!).

A few days before

☐ Grocery shop to cook and freeze a few favorite meals for new parents.

☐ Find out the name and telephone number of a few local restaurants (near the new parents) that deliver.

- Italian: _____
- Mexican: _____
- Greek: _____

- Japanese: _____
- Chinese: _____
- Deli (sandwiches): _____
- Pizza: _____
- Bagels/Bakery: _____

☐ Have phone charged and with you at all times.

☐ Gas up car.

☐ Keep CALM!

Day of baby's arrival

☐ Have phone charged and with you at ALL times! THIS IS YOUR ONE JOB TODAY!

Days following baby's arrival

☐ Have phone with you at all times to answer emergency questions and concerns from the new parents.

☐ Be on-call for emergency questions and concerns from the new parents.

☐ Bring your son or daughter's baby book to the new parents so they can see how they grew.

☐ Drop off prepared meals.

☐ Schedule food deliveries—groceries and/or meals.

☐ Bring over coffee/tea, fruit, bagels, or doughnuts as an AM pick-me-up for the new parents.

☐ Be readily available at a moment's notice.

GRANDPA'S PLAYBOOK

Every winning team has an amazing coach or strong leader who understands their players' characteristics—their personalities, beliefs, motivations, interests, and perceptions—and carefully works strategically on their playbook to ensure a successful team.

As a new grandpa or a grandpa-to-be, your success will be determined by carefully examining your family's characteristics and creating your new "Grandpa's Playbook."

The following guide will assist you with understanding the parents-to-be characteristics and provide suggested advice for creating your own customized playbook. Your playbook is your own guide to becoming a well-loved and respected grandpa!

Parents-to-Be Category and Characteristics	Grandpa's Playbook
Millennial • Technically savvy • "Me" generation • Likes to travel • Life experiences are important • Gets parenting advice ONLINE	Get an iPad ASAP and practice Facetiming with your friends! Speak your mind! They will either listen or completely disregard; they will take no offense. Texting is the best way to communicate with them. Be supportive; offer babysitting.
Gen Y • Cool Mom • Remembers MTV • Husband/dad-to-be helps out	Know the latest and greatest baby products—be hip! Reminisce about the '80s and '90s. Ask the DAD if he needs help or relief— score big here! Be available.

Helicopter

- Pays extreme attention to educational development

- Overschedules

- Dislikes unpleasant or challenging situations for child

Speak only when spoken to—offer no unsolicited advice!

Have unscripted, fun-spirited outings with grandchild.

When alone with grandchild, encourage independent thinking.

No Disney-animated movies or books

Educational book reading only

Tiger	Be kind and gentle when approaching.
• Can be overly protective	Always bring food when visiting.
• Can be authoritative	Ensure parent of your safe environment for grandkids.
	Respect rules, but quietly tell stories to grandkids of "how it used to be back in the day."
Snowplow	Stay out of their way!
• Removes all roadblocks for child	Leave the parenting to the parents.
• May have delusional Princess or Prince thoughts about child	Schedule one-on-one time for normal, fun-time activities with grandpa.
	Be understanding.

DOS, DON'TS, AND ADVICE

Review the following tips to ensure effective communication with the new parents—let's make sure your Grandfatherhood journey gets off to a GREAT start!

DO THIS:

- Offer (don't insist) to babysit.
- Help around the house—fold laundry, load the dishwasher, take out the trash and recycling.
- Walk and feed the dog.
- Pay attention to the other grandchildren.
- Voice no opinions. If you aren't asked for one, don't offer one up. Ever.
- Run a few errands—grocery store, pharmacy, farmers market.

- Take pictures, but don't post pictures without permission.

- Ogle over the baby.

- Be supportive from a distance.

- Know your boundaries.

- Tell the new parents they're doing a great job.

DON'T DO THIS:

- Don't clean up the house without asking first.

- Don't give unsolicited advice.

- If you are given a key to their home, use it sparingly.

- Don't drop in without calling or texting.

- Don't assume that you'll be invited along on trips and vacations

- Don't expect to be invited to every party and social occasion.

- Don't ask about the "next one."

- Don't overwhelm with excessive amounts of gifts.

- Don't withhold your love.

ADVICE:

Grandfathers are still the reliable, go-to source for tried-and-true advice! Here are a few truisms that grandfathers still swear by today:

- Don't take your family for granted.

- Shoulders back, chin up.
- Don't be afraid to fail or lose at anything you chose to do in life.
- If you are not 10 minutes early, you're late.
- Stay honest and keep your integrity.
- If you don't have anything nice to say, don't say it at all.
- Don't grow up too fast.
- Everything in moderation.
- Be nice to your siblings; in the end that's all you'll have.
- This too shall pass.
- Believe in yourself and think positively.
- Sometimes less is more.
- Everything happens for a reason.
- Don't say "goodbye," just "see you later."

NOTES

_____

_____

_____

_____

_____

_____

_____

_____

_____

_____

_____

_____

_____

_____

The Best Grandfather Names Ever

The Best Grandfather Names Ever

The Best Grandfather Names Ever

The Best Grandfather Names Ever

The Best Grandfather Names Ever

The Best Grandfather Names Ever

The Best Grandfather Names Ever

The Best Grandfather Names Ever

The Best Grandfather Names Ever

The Best Grandfather Names Ever

MEMORIES

The Best Grandfather Names Ever

The Best Grandfather Names Ever

ACKNOWLEDGMENTS

First, to my mother "Bubbe," for her unwavering and steadfast determination to claim her rightful grandmother name.

To my children, Kelly Ann and Will, who lived through mounds of papers everywhere and hours of seemingly endless writing and editing. Without their love, support, and understanding, I would have never completed this book.

To my fun, adventurous friend Cathy Swett, who designed the fabulous grandma drawings for my first, self-published book edition.

To my neighbor and literary expert, Nancy Perlman, who unselfishly gave of her time to guide me through this complicated literary process.

To every friend and friend-of-friend who took the time to tell me their wonderful grandmother names and stories. It is because of your generosity this book is true and authentic.

Lastly, to everyone who ever asked me, "How's your book coming along?" It truly inspired and encouraged me to keep going and greatly motivated me to finish this project. For that and more, I am so grateful.

INDEX

ABOUT
THE AUTHOR

Cathy Livingstone believes that today's grandmothers are women-on-the-go, working hard, playing hard, and looking good. She grew up west of Boston (Belmont, MA) and received her computer science degree from The College of William and Mary (Williamsburg, VA). Her work has been featured in the *Washington Post*, *Grand Magazine*, and *Oklahoma Lifestyles 50+*. She currently resides in Montclair, New Jersey.